11 BURNING QUESTIONS ANSWERED ON KEEPING YOUR FAMILY CONNECTED WHEN MONEY MATTERS

BHAJ TOWNSEND

DISCLAIMER AND/OR LEGAL NOTICES
While all attempts have been made to verify information provided in this book and its ancillary materials, neither the author nor publisher assumes any responsibility for errors, inaccuracies or omissions and is not responsible for any financial loss by customers in any manners. Any slights of people or organizations are unintentional. If advice concerning legal, financial, accounting or related matters in needed, the services of a qualified professional should be sought. This book and its associated ancillary materials, including verbal and written training, in not intended for use as a source of legal, financial or accounting advice. You should be aware of the various laws governing business transactions or other business practices in your particular geographic location.

The author has made every effort to ensure the accuracy of the information within this book was correct at time of publication. The author does not assume and hereby disclaims any liability to any party for any loss, damage, or disruption caused by errors or omissions, whether such errors or omissions result from accident, negligence, or any other cause.

Any examples, stories, references or case studies are for illustrative purposes only and should not be interpreted as testimonies and/or examples of what reader and/or consumers can expect. Any statements, strategies, concepts, techniques, exercises and ideas in this information, materials and/or seminar training offered are simply opinion or experience, and thus should not be misinterpreted as promises.

ISBN: 978-0-578-23754-1

To all families who not only understand that it is as important to prepare the family as it is to prepare the money for its eventual transfer, but then actually commit to creating the family environment that transfers wisdom with wealth for generations.

And to Francie, Dawn, and Gordon for their guidance and support in bringing this book to life.

CONTENTS

WELCOME

If you are reading this book, then you may already understand that there is a decision to make about the future of your family.

It is a decision that will impact the longevity of your family's harmony, reaching way beyond the financial wealth you have built. This harmony will encompass purpose, trust, and unity as your family's wealth grows and is then transferred from generation to generation. As the revered consultant and researcher, Roy Williams, of the Williams Group, found when he studied and worked with families of wealth, trust, communication, and respect go a long way toward sustaining a family. Its members feel confident and prepared as the baton of leadership is passed from one generation to the next.

As you transfer your wealth, your family will have challenges to overcome and decisions to make to keep it unified. Some of these challenges, you will find, you can overcome yourself, while others will need the expertise of those who can guide you in building the sense of trust and harmony that will help your family thrive.

As you build a family that can develop unity across generations, you will learn to distinguish wisdom from folly and patience from expedience. Doing so will serve you and your family well.

Becoming a long-lasting family takes commitment, determination, and a keen sense of purpose built on F.A.M.E.: flexibility, accountability, measurability, and empathy. May you build a family that will live long—because you have transferred wisdom with wealth.

When I received my inheritance at age twenty-one, I had no idea what to do with it.

My fifty-cent childhood allowances hadn't prepared me for the big check—a check that quickly removed me from the world of small and insignificant purchases. What was I to do with this new money? I really had no idea, other than spend it. But I did not want to do that. I felt I was given this gift to do more with it. I just did not know what. So I deposited the check in the bank.

Because money was left to me by my dad, who had passed away ten years earlier, I felt there must be a purpose to this inheritance, although no note or instruction had been left for me regarding its use. I did not want to blow it. But none of my four older brothers or my mother wanted to engage in conversations about inheritances. It was a forbidden subject, which left me to ponder questions about money's purpose, its worth, what beneficiaries were supposed to do with their money, what beneficiaries actually did, and how wealthy families talked about money.

So, as a young adult, with no guidance on how to productively steward my own inheritance, I began to study wealthy families and their relationships with money. I wanted to know:

- How do families talk about money?
- Do siblings talk to each other about inherited money?
- Does something happen to family cohesion once money is transferred from one generation to the next?
- How do beneficiaries view their inheritance? Do they suddenly feel different from others? Do they hide their wealth, flaunt it, spend it, invest it, give it away?
- What happens when or if beneficiaries run out of money?
- What happens if one sibling goes through the inherited money and needs more but another does not?
- Is money an "elephant in the room" for wealthy families? If so, what are the consequences?

As I studied the impact of wealth on families, I discovered that although they were certainly delighted to receive their inheritances, beneficiaries really did not know how to think about this money, other than as "secret" money. This meant that they did not generally talk to their siblings or to the remaining parent about it. If they did, the discussion was often short and awkward. Beneficiaries, by and large, felt most comfortable spending or hiding their money. Often, their actions stemmed from feelings of inadequacy about their ability to handle large sums of money. Sometimes they felt they did not do anything to deserve their inheritance. Often, they felt they could not meet the assumed expectations that came with this wealth.

You may have heard of beneficiaries who spent or squandered their inheritances. Research has found that seventy percent of (inherited) family wealth is gone by the end of the second generation (this means by the death of the wealth-creator's children) and nincty percent of inherited family wealth is gone by the end of the third generation (the wealth-creator's grandchildren).

Will your family become another data point in this startling statistic? Most probably, unless you do something proactive to prevent it from happening to you.

Fortunately, there *are* families who thrive with family money. One of the longest established legacy families owns the Hoshi Hotel in Japan, which has been run by the same family for more than forty generations. Yes, forty generations! You may have heard of the Rothschilds, a cohesive and thriving family for more than seven generations, or the Tennessee-based Bush family, now in its fifth generation of business and family leadership.

What is it about these families that keeps them united? What keeps them harmonious when money becomes the great divider in so many other families—in fact, in the vast majority of families—with wealth?

After much study, I learned that there were several key elements common to families who are able to stay connected. They have a sense of common purpose, mission, shared values, and a feeling of belonging to a meaningful culture—families who retained their money and family harmony generation after generation. You will hear about these elements in the following pages.

From my search for what worked to keep families united, I dedicated my professional life to providing the formula for families who want to become stewards of both their family money and their own individual wealth. I have implemented processes and systems that provide platforms for family members to stay cohesive as they develop the longer-term purposes of their family, their wealth, and learn to develop a community of ongoing trust and leadership across generations. Over time, I have seen families transform their messy dynamics to dynamics of trust, and I've watched as they join the ranks of successful, continuing legacy families.

This guidebook contains my responses to eleven of the most vexing questions that families with wealth encounter and must resolve:

1. How can we prevent our kids from squandering the money?
2. When and how do we teach our kids about financial literacy and the value of money?
3. How do we create meaning for the family money?
4. How does legacy planning differ from estate planning?
5. How do we build the basis of a legacy family?
6. What is the benefit of having annual family meetings?
7. How can we make family meetings more interesting?
8. How do we keep our new financial status from undermining family harmony?
9. How can we deepen trust within the family?

10. How can we spark future generations' interest in the family business?
11. What should we consider in hiring someone to guide us in developing our family legacy?

I have set out to make sure that this guidebook will benefit you by:

- Serving as a launch pad for thought, motivation, and planning as you build a strong sense of family financial stewardship that can be passed on to your children, your grandchildren, their children, and so on.
- Serving as a cornucopia of ideas and possibilities for you and your family, as you strive to successfully transform your initial financial accumulation into long-term stewardship for your family for generations to come.
- Serving as a guide as you consider what you can do to keep your family strong and harmonious when money is a key element of your family dynamics.
- I hope this guidebook enables you to keep your family cohesive for at least 100 years, because money and family matter, together.

1

HOW CAN WE PREVENT OUR KIDS FROM SQUANDERING THE MONEY?

This is not a new question. In fact, it is one that has plagued families for centuries. Inherent in the question is a wish that inherited money will continue to benefit the family in ways that contribute to the next generation's growth and happiness, without interfering with their independence, drive, motivation, and self-determination. The question really means: are my kids ready to steward their inheritance?

Your concerns about the next generation's ability to take on the responsibility of stewarding their inherited wealth are not unusual. You may wonder whether they can comfortably (or intelligently) handle large sums, or whether they will squander the money. You may worry that they will spend it on too many impulse buys. So, what can you do to allay your fears and prepare your heirs for their wealth?

Many people simply have their estate attorneys draw up trust documents that prohibit children from acquiring their inherited money until the arrival of set dates or predetermined milestones. However, statistics and real-life examples show that even with the best-designed estate documents, families still manage to spend down and even squander their wealth. Legal documents may keep the money around a little longer, but these well-prepared documents do little, if anything, to prepare inheritors to steward their inheritances. Hopes and assumptions do not prepare future generations for their own web of emotions and ensuing responsibilities regarding money.

You may have heard stories in the media about squandered financial legacies, among them the inherited wealth of Barbara Hutton, heiress of two financial empires, F.W. Woolworth and E.F. Hutton; Anthony Marshall, heir to the Astor fortune; or many others who were given so much yet were mentored so little. For them, money made it easier to ignore or abdicate their responsibilities. They were not taught to become stewards of a financial legacy or stewards of a family story and shared purpose. Thus, their vast inheritances did not make it to the next generation.

Instead of continuing this cycle of squandering wealth, families need to provide a framework for inheritors to understand the roles and responsibilities they must learn about and undertake when wealth is given to them. Inheritors need to understand the purpose of family money—and this is key—as distinct from their own individually earned money.

When the presence of money is assumed, or is seen as relatively easy to acquire from a preceding generation, it can be difficult to believe that it will not *always* be there. That does not suggest that the solution is to keep money away from heirs. That can breed contempt or resentment. Instead, it is important to talk about money. But how do you do so without potential outbursts or unintended innuendos hovering over relationships?

That key point above—about distinguishing between inherited family money and individually earned money—is critical. Family money is the money that has been set aside for common and shared purposes. Individual money is the money that individuals accumulate and earn to support their own independent objectives and lifestyles; it is separate and distinct from family money.

Ask yourself this: "What is this 'family money' for?" What is its purpose? Will it fund educational pursuits, provide down payments for first homes, become loans for business, entrepreneurial seed funding, support for a family member's personal development or exceptional medical needs, maintain a family vacation home, pay off credit cards, develop philanthropic initiatives? Whatever the intention(s), it is important to determine the purpose of family money. When this is carefully and thoughtfully expressed and recorded, family members can understand and adhere to its purpose. The purpose for the family money will help them understand the clear differences between what their own individual earnings are for and what the family money is for, without expecting to comingle these funds or have them serve one another.

This dichotomy innately provides a framework of distinction between common and individual money. When this distinction is defined, family members understand when to bring up family wealth and the conversations to support its development, and understand how to distinguish this family money from their own individual money for their own lifestyles.

Rightfully so, most parents do not want to see their children or grandchildren feel entitled to their money. They think such an attitude could produce lazy or rudderless children. But this could easily happen if nothing has been put in place to guide the children in understanding the purpose of the family money and, at the same time, the purpose of their own money, with an understanding that each will carry its own distinct roles and responsibilities.

When new generations grow up with the understanding that family money is not available or meant to serve each person's individual whims and wants, future heirs will be more motivated to build their own lives and earn their own money to support their chosen lifestyles. They will not simply live in anticipation of the day when they will receive their inheritance and thus fail to create their own future. They will become stewards of the family money while building their own lives. This kind of thoughtful planning needs to be integrated into the family culture, rather than added as edicts once the inheritors reach a certain age where they might not be prepared to take on the responsibilities expected of them.

One way to encourage integration into the family culture is to talk frequently about money and its purpose within your family. Start early and build activities that develop and acknowledge productive and sustainable financial behaviors. Doing so will give your children the best chance to learn and use beneficial habits and behaviors with money. Provide activities and opportunities to save, invest, donate, earn, and spend their own money while understanding and supporting the purpose of the family money.

When your children and grandchildren, as well as their children and grandchildren, are prepared and well-equipped to become financial stewards, you will not have to worry about them becoming squanderers or spenders of your wealth. They will have tools that develop a greater understanding of the role of family money, which they, in turn, can pass on to their children.

2

WHEN AND HOW DO WE TEACH OUR KIDS ABOUT FINANCIAL LITERACY AND THE VALUE OF MONEY?

Money conversations need not stay locked in silence, only to emerge later in directives or short instructional messages. It is important to talk often about money at home so that, over time, your fears about how your children or grandchildren will use your well-earned money will diminish.

At an Ivy League school alumni dinner I attended, the host asked the attendees to indicate, by a show of hands, whether they had engaged in financial discussions with their children and/or grandchildren on a monthly or more frequent basis? Of the 100 attendees, only THREE hands went up!

What does this tell us? That few families are deliberate in their approach to talking about money at home. For many families, money is a difficult subject to discuss because it is often viewed differently by each parent. Their unique backgrounds, as well as cultural and childhood experiences, impact their perspectives on money.

Each of us has stories about money stemming from our early childhood experiences with it. We carry these stories with us into adulthood. What we heard about money, how we were taught about money (if we were), how we were told to talk about money, what we did with money we received, and more, carry forward into how we interact with money as adults.

Money often creates an emotionally charged atmosphere in families where there is wealth and this can become polarizing. One parent may want to be generous with the children when it comes to money, while another wants to set strict guidelines. One may want to talk about money in front of the children, while another avoids the conversation altogether. In the presence of divergent behaviors money can become a difficult subject.

Although seventeen American states require a personal finance "course" to be taken in high school, only five states require a stand-alone semester on financial topics before graduation. Money, a commodity we all use and are responsible for, is rarely taught. Even in schools where I have taught elective classes on money, it has been unusual to find students who were comfortable having conversations about money with their parents. In my classes, students did not know how to talk to their parents about credit, loans, how to deal with peer spending pressures, or how to allocate money to saving, investing, spending, or giving. Money was a mystery to them although they were "sure" they could invest money and make money quickly in the stock market. Most money conversations were among friends about how their parents did not understand their needs for money or trust them with money.

It is up to you to introduce financial literacy at home, even when you and your spouse perceive money differently. You must create an environment where money is treated coherently rather than surrounded by mystery or consequential innuendo. Money needs to be discussed in an environment of exploration, discovery, adventure, and guidance.

Here are a few suggestions based on both my experiences and on accredited research on this vexing topic of financial literacy for children:

- **Three-to-six-year-old children** can be introduced to money directly and early. Have them collect coins and sort them into various sizes. Have them count money as an arithmetic exercise. Get them accustomed to handling real money. Make money tangible. Having an early and repeated exposure to real money gives children a relationship with it. The key here is to familiarize children in this age group with actual currency (coins and paper) so they themselves interact with money and have their own direct experience with it. Observe your children with money. Watch them experience it. Be informal yet let your children see money, touch money, count money, talk about their experiences with money, and have them ask you questions about money. Let them see you use money.
- **Five-to-seven-year-old children** love games as they begin to accept early responsibilities. Games that involve bartering are great activities for this age group. Have them barter with you for an item at home you think would be appropriate for them to learn about, regarding the benefits of trading. This is an appropriate age to introduce children to piggy banks.

(Remember piggy banks?!) They are still around today, and they are a great tool for learning how money can be saved and used. There are piggy banks with storage sections for saving, spending, donating, and investing. Your children can decide how much they want to allocate to each section and what they want to use the money for in those sections. They can see and experience the consequences of holding onto or depleting one of their sections. They can determine strategies for building them back up. Another suggestion: Have children choose items at a grocery store and pay for these items with cash. Observe their reactions as they receive change back. What do they want to do with that change? Money is personal and tends to elicit an emotional response. We feel a sense of loss when we surrender actual cash for a purchase, whereas our brains do not register the same way when we use credit cards. On another trip to the grocery store, have them pay with a credit card. Observe their reactions there. A credit card is abstract for a child. Although there is money owed, the brain does not register a change in financial conditions; it does not register a reduction of money with a card. It is not real to the part of the brain that senses this type of change.

- **Eight-to-eleven-year-old children** are especially ready to experience limits to making choices. Next time you go shopping with your children, ask them what kind of choices they are going to make on items they want to buy. Have them talk about the impact their choices will have on the money in their piggy banks or saving accounts. Be aware that they are accustomed to the lifestyle in which they are being raised and tend to mimic it. If you want them to set limits for themselves and make thoughtful choices, they must observe you modeling that behavior. For them to be told one thing while seeing you modeling another makes it difficult for them to know what they should do. If you keep telling them they can't spend limitlessly, yet they see or hear conversations at home only about spending, your children may well be confused about what the real money message is.

- **Preteens** love to feel responsible. This is a great time to introduce your kids to budgets. They learn to navigate between what they *want* to purchase and what they *can* purchase. When done in a supportive learning and experiential framework, they gain confidence. They can begin to talk about their experiences. They learn about the ramifications and consequences of exceeding budgets, and this will contribute to their sense of autonomy with money. When they exceed their budgets, use these experiences as learning opportunities. Ask them how they will approach the next thing for which they are budgeting. Ask them how they share expenses with their friends. The main point here is to talk to them about their use of money, not as a judge, but as a guide. Help them talk about their money. Let them be confused and make mistakes, and then help them learn from those mistakes. Acknowledge them for good behaviors and for beneficial changes they make after a mistake they've made.
- **Teens** feel peer pressure. The need to belong can tug hard at their financial behaviors. It can be a deterrent to setting financial limits and boundaries. "But you don't understand, I need this…now!" is a common plea. This is a wonderful time to introduce the concept of earning money away from home. You can also introduce teens to the concept of investing. First,

find out what they know about investing, if anything, and what they think investing will do for them. Then, experiment by having them choose a stock they would invest in and—without actually investing in that stock—watch it with them for a few months. Have them talk about their feelings as the stock languishes, drops, and rises. This is also an appropriate time to introduce them to the family business by taking them to the company and introducing them to the financially responsible staff in each department. Begin conversations about the family money. They are already aware of its existence and now is a beneficial time for them to learn about its purpose and to understand their own roles and responsibilities with this money.

- **Young adults** are spreading their wings and testing the boundaries of their independent lives. They are often thrown into a world that feels like being on a financial tightrope, one on which they feel wobbly and unprepared to walk. They want this, they need that. How do they decide between the two? Because some young adults may have feelings of guilt or shame about money or even about their inability to add to their family's financial success, they may express these insecurities by binge spending, or helping to pay for their friends' lifestyles, or at the other extreme, by hiding from their family's money and pretending it does not exist. This is the time for young adults, if they haven't already, to learn what money means to them and to set up a system they can follow to save, invest, donate, earn, and spend. The purpose of the family money, along with their roles and responsibilities with it, should all be well-defined so there is a clear distinction between what their own (earned) money is for and what the family money is for.

As you introduce money conversations and money stewardship at home, remember to guide and advise rather than dictate; encourage rather than criticize; and be consistent, flexible, objective, and purposeful about money. Keep extended family members—aunts and uncles, godparents and grandparents—in the loop about your financial "rules," encourage accountability, and praise successes. Be open to your children's questions, mistakes, and ideas. Let money become another conversation that encourages and fosters ideas for building financial stewardship.

Without a foundation for financial competence, people run the risk of squandering, overspending, or squabbling over money. Money can create tension among spouses and between generations. Instead, when children have experience with money early, they can discover, tweak, and learn from their decisions, mistakes, and challenges. This is how they will become intelligent stewards of money.

Discuss and explore money in ways that foster understanding and respect between generations. Start talking about money, its purpose, its challenges, its five essential components (save, invest, donate, earn, and spend), and the opportunities each component provides.

3

HOW DO WE CREATE MEANING AND PURPOSE FOR THE FAMILY MONEY?

When asked about the impact money would have on the lives of their heirs, 65% of respondents in one study said there would be too much attention on material things, 55% said their heirs would stay naïve about the value of money, 52% said their heirs would spend beyond their means, and 50% said that their heirs' initiatives would be ruined by money. This suggests that money without a dedicated purpose is fraught with minefields.

The conclusion is clear: There is concern about wealth passing successfully from one generation to the next. Twenty-plus years of my own observation and experience have certainly confirmed this.

Although you may understand and value the money you have amassed, your children and grandchildren most likely do not share your views about your money. How could they? They have a different approach to money. With their unique perspectives and agendas, they see the money you have accumulated through the lens of their own needs and wants, experiences, and filters.

Your children and grandchildren will tend to push for their own individual needs and agendas with your money. Each individual's projects and claims are felt to be as important, if not more important, than those of their siblings. Tension between siblings may even create stress on you and your spouse as you argue about financial considerations.

From both my own experience and my work with families in developing financial literacy, I have found that establishing a purpose for the family money is essential to creating and sustaining harmony in the family. It provides a foundation of understanding and agreement regarding the family money and will help to clarify that family money is not meant simply to satisfy specific individual needs.

To help you approach the topic of defining the purpose of family money, here are some guidelines:

1. First, dedicate time to thinking about what you want your money to provide for your heirs one, two, three, or five generations into the future. How do you want this money to benefit them? Write a paragraph or two describing what it took for you to amass your wealth. Include in your story the challenges and setbacks you faced and how you successfully dealt with them. Describe what it means to you to have accumulated your wealth. How do you see your wealth benefiting future generations? Future generations—those who are further removed from the origins of family wealth—will want to know. It will help them feel connected

to its meaning, its origins, and to their roles as stewards of something important.

2. Second, schedule a family meeting during which you can discuss and reach an understanding with your family about the purpose of the money, describing what it is to you and hearing what it means to them. Once everybody has had an opportunity to hear and reflect upon the purpose of the family money, family members can and will more easily honor the boundaries around it.

From this foundation, your family will be ready to initiate and develop activities that support cohesion around the use of the family money. These activities might include: developing family philanthropic goals and initiatives, and hosting workshops that build intergenerational connections on topics like: determining which organizations to support, how various generations view money, communication that fosters harmony—to name a few. These will help teach young children about using their money and build a structured approach that introduces younger generations to the family business and how its finances intersect with the purposes of the family.

Your wealth can become a great resource for your family, serving a common purpose spanning many generations. Develop and introduce activities that support the purpose of the family money.

When we prepare an estate plan for the eventual transfer of our assets, we tend to think primarily about who gets what and when they are entitled to it. But is this really enough to ensure a successful transfer of assets?

Preparing assets for eventual distribution is not enough preparation if a family is to remain cohesive for generations. Why? Because simply preparing the money for distribution does not prepare the inheritors to become responsible recipients and stewards of the money. It does not prepare their emotions for the possible differences in distribution among siblings. It does not prepare them to understand their role in terms of the role you want them to consider with their inheritance. Preparation is the key for both assets and beneficiaries.

We've already seen that for a large percentage of families who pass their assets from one generation to the next, the inherited money is often gone by the end of the second generation and, in many instances, family members have drifted apart. You may think it is the money itself that keeps family members connected. But money itself does not. Money is merely a commodity. It is the squandering, squabbling, or unwise spending that breaks a family apart. So preparing for the inheritors' needs goes hand-in-hand with preparing the money.

Families, like organizations, tend to fall apart when there is no agreed-upon or understood purpose for staying together or there is no magnetic leader. Without a unifying purpose, a family's natural tendency is to become a group of people with competing agendas and bickering factions rather than one built around harmony and agreed-upon missions and shared initiatives. Instead of building a team that develops a harmonious future, the family finds itself losing contact with one another, going separate ways, losing links to its own culture and core. Your family's purpose is the glue that keeps your family unified.

As you will find in Chapter 5, families find the process of crafting a mission statement to be powerful. Because members are jointly deciding on their "reason for being," they often find a new sense of harmony and camaraderie. With a commonly supported mission and purpose, family members are assured that they have a place at the table and can bring ideas and value to the conversation. Having a family mission statement can also help maintain family harmony as the family expands and new members join.

Many new companies, organizations, and even countries devise their own mission statements. It is the core statement to which they can refer for years to come, even as leaders change. Expect to see the dynamics of your own family strengthen during your money conversations, as you establish your own purpose-driven mission statement.

4

HOW CAN WE SPARK FUTURE GENERATIONS' INTEREST IN THE FAMILY BUSINESS?

As you study the next generations' involvement in the family business I recommend that you consider a three-step process that will trigger and identify their interests, as well as their ideal roles and responsibilities.

Step One: Introduce the next generation to the vision and mission of the business at an early age. Casually introduce them to various parts of the business to see what, if anything, interests them. Watch what they question and are drawn to, so you can understand what they want to explore and what they want to learn about the business. Listen to how their views and visions of the future are distinct from your own. Let them know what the business means to you, both as a business and as a family asset. Let them know what motivated you, or those who came before you, to start the business. Listen to what questions this sparks in your children. Have them watch you as you work in the business. Involve them when they are young in order to see what they gravitate to. People tend to pursue what motivates them personally.

Step Two: Determine who best fits into various roles and responsibilities, rather than assigning them on the basis of age, gender, or favoritism. Some families put their work-age children into roles in which they are not reporting directly to their parents, enabling the child to build confidence and a rapport with others. Give them room to grow and move up without compromising the integrity of the company.

Other families take a different approach. They have their children intern and work in other businesses to acquire an understanding of what it is to be a non-family member employee and to understand that working in the family business is not an obligation, but a privilege, alongside all other employees.

Step Three: Formalize procedures for your family members so they know their roles, their responsibilities, the structure of command, and expectations. Create an environment where they can feel comfortable and free to share their experiences and perspectives without fear of criticism or personal reprisal. Listen to their ideas so they can feel heard.

You may find that not every family member is as excited about the business as you are. And certainly, not everyone in successive generations will want to join the family business. Honor their decisions, as difficult as this may be. You want what is best for the business. You want what is best for the family.

Although I did not include this as a step, keep in mind that family and business are separate, but overlapping entities. When conducting business, stay away from family dynamics and family topics. When home, stay away from business discussions. If there are family members not active in the family business, they will feel isolated if the family gathering keeps returning to the family business. Following this model can give you tremendous dividends in preventing collisions between non-business and business members of the family. Knowing how to separate family from the family business is essential to keeping harmony.

Generational Perspectives on the Family Business

A family business is a unique entity. The founding generation has likely sacrificed a great deal to make the business a success. But succeeding generations may see things quite differently.

I first heard the concept of "generational perspectives" when I heard Tom Rogerson, former senior managing director and family wealth strategist at Wilmington Trust Company, describe the term. He said that the first generation provides the driving, visionary decision-making and entrepreneurial acumen. Initially, the focus of the business is scattered. The founders dedicate themselves to the business, meeting challenges and forging successes. This is, in essence, their "baby."

The second generation, generally speaking, is brought up with more resources at their disposal, they are generally more educated, and they may have had experience in the business under their parents' direction. The second generation tends to be more systems oriented in their approach than the first generation. They tend to be more procedural and more managerial.

As the third generation grows up, they are usually in an environment comfortable with the wealth that has been accumulated from the business. The third generation is further removed from the business's creation and startup challenges. "It's always been here," is their perception. "It runs like a well-oiled machine," is their experience. A third generation's mind is usually more creative than it is entrepreneurial.

It is critical that each generation understand the perspectives of the others. Succeeding generations must be given the opportunity to participate in the business where they can contribute their ideas, develop their own unique skills, visions, and strategies, alongside the values and mission of the business, without undue constraint. With corresponding talents and skills aligned with the values and mission of the business, the next generations will likely be better prepared, respected, trusted, and emboldened in moving the business forward and continuing its legacy and success.

For those who would like to delve further into the intergenerational dynamics of a family and its family business, my book, ***Build a Lasting Legacy***, focuses on one family with a member who does not interact or take part in the family business. You may find this book helpful, especially in the chapters that address next generations who show great interest, some interest, and lack of interest in the family business.

5

HOW DOES LEGACY PLANNING DIFFER FROM ESTATE PLANNING?

Legacy planning is a key component to estate planning. While estate planning takes care of transferring assets from one generation to the next, legacy planning ensures that the family is able to steward its wealth and carry on the family mission, while keeping members and generations connected and harmonious.

For centuries, estate planning has benefited families and businesses by employing strategies that protect and distribute assets to subsequent generations. Techniques and strategies for doing this have been developed and refined to ensure that assets and tangible property are distributed as intended, while also keeping the family harmonious and unified. Intricate strategies have allowed family assets to be transferred tax-favorably and privately, away from the prying eyes of the media and of those excluded from the plan. Estate planning has become an essential tool in effectively safeguarding assets during their transfer from one generation to the next.

But estate planning is not the same as legacy planning! While assets are being carefully safeguarded and purposefully distributed, how are the ***beneficiaries*** being prepared to receive these assets and steward them with care? This is an important question, since studies have shown dire consequences for the vast majority of families of inherited wealth. A full seventy percent of families lose their wealth by the end of the second generation and ninety percent of families have lost their wealth by the end of the third generation. NOT statistics to aspire to!

It appears that while those with wealth carefully plan their estates, many fail to create the essential legacy that creates the platform and culture of stewardship of wealth. When beneficiaries do not know how to steward their inherited wealth, they tend to squander it and/or fight over it, either among themselves or with their trust officers. What is not said here but is a familiar theme: the family's harmony will have succumbed to disruption.

In essence, legacy planning prepares family members for their roles as stewards of their inheritance, both as individuals and as an intentional community of like-minded members and family culture keepers. They become stewards of money for the next generation who in turn become stewards for the next generation and so forth. There is a long view to their wealth.

Legacy planning involves the implementation of systems and activities that can be sustained for generations to keep the family wealth strong and harmonious. (We'll be going into these in greater detail in Chapter 7.)

Legacy families are those families who intentionally put processes and tools in place to develop harmony in their family over generations. Just as a country with a constitution, or a business with a purpose and mission, a legacy family creates its own constitution or mission that is relevant and significant to that particular family. Looking at the origin of the word "legacy," according to the Online Etymology Dictionary, the word stems both from 14th century French: "legate-body of persons sent on a mission," and from the Middle Latin "ambassador or envoy."

Fortunately, a legacy family is not a new concept. There are long-standing legacy families around the world. You have probably heard of a few, such as the Rothschilds, the Rockefellers, and the Bushs (of the bean fortune). You may not have heard of other families who have committed to keeping their families intact, like the Nortons, Wrights, Fishers, and Pritzkers. And there are the legions of families who have made headlines as their wealth was squandered, squabbled over, or spent until it was a mere shadow of its former self. The families who have continued to thrive have done so by forming their purpose, and by creating and keeping relevant their values, mission, and objectives across several generations. They are intentional while continuing to be a family with a unique culture and dynamics. In their success we find hints, clues, and best practices for any family wanting to build a legacy of their own.

Let me introduce you to one such legacy family. You may have heard of or used Kikkoman Soy Sauce; if so, you have indirectly been introduced to the Mogi family. They have remained unified for seventeen generations. Their family creed, which was originally crafted in the seventeenth century, is still revered by members of the family today. It was written over a century ago and is reviewed periodically. It states their purpose and covers the meaning behind their values. Because they have a family business, their creed talks about family conduct in the business. It talks about saving money and loaning to family members. The family understands and experiences the outcome of maintaining their relevance and significance through this creed. They meet as a large group periodically and talk about their purpose; they have meaningful conversations about who they have been in the past, who they are today, and where they want to be in the future. Next time you pick up a Kikkoman Soy Sauce bottle, you might see on the label the year 1630. This family has stayed connected and even more relevant and unified in their purpose since then. Nowadays, rather than resting on their business laurels, the Mogi family updates their creed whenever necessary. Rather than hiding behind their financial success, this family serves a greater community through the vision and mission of a living family purpose.

You may have heard of the Root, Pitcairn, Smith, or Blakely families. Each has committed to staying purposefully unified through many generations. They have clearly defined their purpose, have found and cultivated their shared family values, have established their mission, built intergenerational teams to support their philanthropic drives, and dealt with family issues. They are committed to deepening the trust they know can shatter if not nurtured. They are committed to staying harmonious and unified in flexible and relevant ways with tools and activities that work well for them.

But creating and maintaining a unified purpose and mission can be a challenge. A family I had the opportunity to work with struggled with intergenerational communication and trust. One of the first-generation members felt that the second generation was not ready for leadership roles. The second generation, in turn, was frustrated by their parents' unwillingness to transfer responsibilities to them and by their parents' inability to communicate with them about planning for the future and the eventual transfer of assets. Family get-togethers became increasingly uncomfortable.

In our work together, I facilitated conversations focused on what stewardship and legacy meant to them. As they listened to each other and developed their definitions and descriptions of these concepts, they forged paths of deeper respect for each other and a communal understanding of the purpose of their wealth for the family, as a unit, and to the purpose of the family wealth and its role in the community they wanted to impact. The family realized they wanted to foster bonds that would thrive through and across generations. They began to talk about the meaning of trust. They looked at what success meant to them and what challenges it presented to them as a family. Going through these initial conversations cleared the air of hostility and suspicion; and the facilitated conversations provided a platform on which to build deeper trust and harmony while healing open wounds. With this renewed spirit, they excitedly dove into the exercise of identifying their core family values. With these newly discovered common values as their beacon, they crafted their family constitution. Because this constitution was now their centerpiece of purpose, their behaviors changed. They now had a common point to rally around, and this changed the way they behaved together. Years later, they continue to remark on the difference that was made by going through the process of finding shared values—values they wanted to foster and develop—and how this process had saved them as a family.

In short, for any family to carry on, unified, for generations, it must have a mission or purpose that its members agree upon, support, and continually develop. To achieve this, long-lasting families must first determine their own set of agreed-upon family values, as the family above did. From this strong base, families then create their unique purpose or mission statement, which, as their constitution, becomes the centerpiece that they strive to keep relevant and vibrant, along with creating intergenerational activities that contribute to the meaning of philanthropy for the family. This may encompass the development of philanthropic initiatives and workshops on the meaning of money for the family, along with initiatives to support their meaning, discussions and study of changing technology so the family, as an intergenerational unit, can feel connected, and many other activities. These will help support family members in becoming stewards of a legacy rather than merely being inheritors of wealth.

As noted earlier, legacy planning is a key component of estate planning for families who want to keep themselves united and connected and champions of their common purpose.

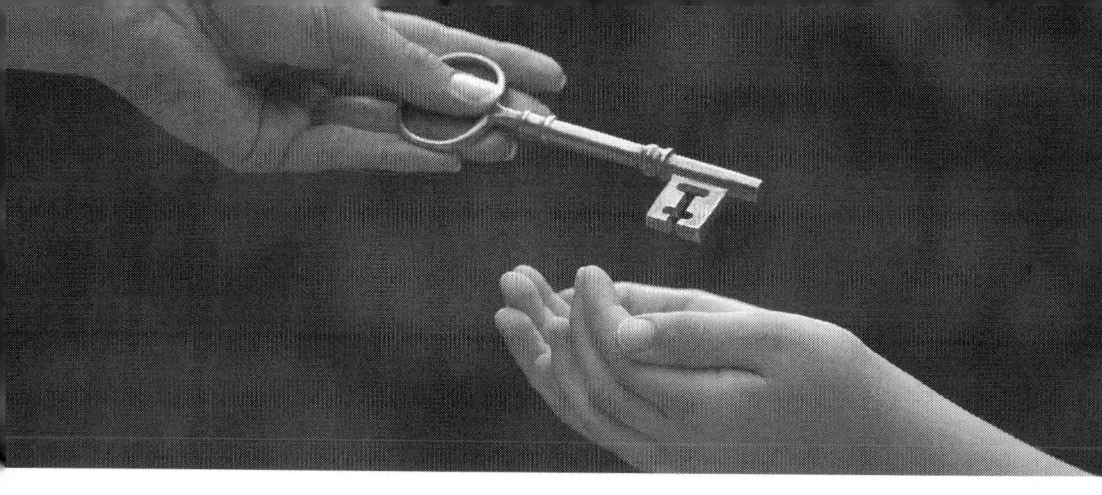

6

HOW DO WE BUILD THE BASIS OF A LEGACY FAMILY?

As we get into how to build a legacy family foundation, let me briefly describe what a legacy family is. A legacy family is one that can:

- Stand united across generations in common purpose and shared values
- Welcome and incorporate new members into its culture
- Respect the voices of all members: young, old, and in between
- Encourage unity while also developing individuality

A legacy family is not built overnight, nor does it represent a static culture. Instead, a family begins by laying the foundation for its sustainability.

There are three key elements that families need to incorporate in building unity and harmony for generations: identifying the family values; recording the family story; and developing a mission statement.

A. Identifying Family Values

The first element is the identification or codifying of family values. This is the first opportunity for the family to determine their core values, the ones they believe tie them together, and represent who they are as a culture and as a brand.

These are the values that represent what you believe in and what matters most to you as a unit. They act as the compass for big decisions you may make, as well as guide how you regard one another and relate to the community you engage with. Your family values originate from the members' contributions, which are then collected and summarized and become the core values the family harmoniously agrees to.

Here are three common approaches to establishing your family's values:

1. **A1:** During a family meeting, family members each identify what they believe the family's core values are. Then, as a group, they discuss and prioritize these values and establish a list of those they agree upon. Everyone's voice will have been heard and acknowledged, and common ground can then be established.
2. **A2:** The founding generation—the generation that seeks to intentionally form a long-lasting legacy family—can tell its story, sharing the inspiration behind their core values and telling how these have helped shape their lives and the larger family culture. The founding generation's values thus become the basis on which to create the family's initial value structure.

3. **A3:** A blend of the two approaches above could involve the founding generation's revelation of their most precious values as the springboard for the family to consider as it develops its own value structure.

Whichever way you choose to define your family values, keep in mind that these values are the foundation, the centerpiece, upon which your family will build and maintain connections for generations. These values represent a why-you-exist as a family. Without identifying this essence of the family, individuals may be left to pursue their own agendas and their own interests, sometimes to the detriment of family harmony and unity.

B. Recording the Family Story

The second element crucial to building the foundation of a legacy family is the recording of the relevant family story. This is the story that will serve as the lodestar for those generations who will never meet the founding generation. An awareness of its own history is critical to a family's legacy.

Keeping connections strong across generations requires knowledge of what it took for the family to get to where it is today. This narrative is much more than a list of relevant dates and timelines. It should reveal what contributed to developing the principles and values that have guided its previous generations' lives.

Dr. Marshall Duke, a researcher, professor of psychology, and a founder of the "Do You Know" Scale at Emory University, explored myths and rituals in the family system in his research (read it here: https://lairdnortonwm.com/wp-content/uploads/Questions-and-Answers-with-Dr.-Marshall-Duke.pdf). He saw that the more children knew about their family's history, the stronger was their sense of control over their own lives, the higher their self-esteem, and the more successfully they believed their families functioned. Belonging to a community in which you have a vested interest with which you are affiliated, and for which you feel an allegiance, creates the feeling of your being part of something bigger than yourself.

There are many ways a family can approach capturing its story. Among the best ways is to bring in a personal historian or biographer who is experienced at asking the questions that will reveal the core of what made the family who they are, including milestones, significant people and events, and ways they met challenges—those important facets behind the information that may be readily available on Google. You will want to be sure that the resulting story is not merely a list of dates and events but also focuses on how challenges were overcome, how values were developed, how these values played a role in overcoming hardships, and how the family built its success. All of this valuable information gives future generations a stronger sense of confidence about who they are and how they can live their own lives while building the strengths and values that contribute to who they will become.

C. Creating a Family Mission Statement

The third foundational element is the development of the family's mission statement. A mission statement can provide a roadmap into what defines the family's reason for being. It becomes the north star, that immovable point of relevance and meaning for the family. A family gains a deeper sense of meaning and connection when they define their own unique mission.

Most families do not have a mission statement. Those families who do craft one have been able to move from individual conversations to group conversations that help develop and support individual strengths and skills for the benefit of the entire family. They feel a deeper sense of collaboration with each other and exhibit less competition among themselves. They know where the family is going (based on where it has been), and they understand and agree with the plan for going forward.

Here are two suggested steps for creating a family mission statement:

1. **C1:** Gather the family for a group conversation about what really matters to them as a cohesive unit. Find out what each individual family member believes is important about the family as a whole. You will undoubtedly hear unique perspectives about what each member thinks and about where the family should develop as a unit. You may also hear interesting ideas framed as actual initiatives or even as things the family shouldn't do. These are all pertinent, but the crux of this conversation will be to establish the values that bind and connect your family together as a unit.
2. **C2:** Once you have determined the family values, your next step is to craft a mission or purpose statement. This is your family's expression of what you represent. Your strengths and values are huge elements in your mission, since they embody the family's motivations. This is an opportunity to ask: What do we, as a family, stand for? What do we, as a family, want to create and then develop for generations?

When you formalize your mission statement, you set the direction and purpose for your family for generations to come. With your values and mission in hand, you have a foundation on which to build structures and teams to lead the family forward in expressing its mission. Perhaps you will develop a philanthropic team, or a group that will put together the agenda for next year's meeting. Perhaps you will create workshops on financial literacy, on communication, on integrating new partners or spouses into the family, or on mentoring next generations into the culture of the bigger purpose.

Family values, the initial family story, and family's mission are not static elements that are created once and never looked at again. Each generation of a true legacy family will add to these elements, making sure they are still relevant and keeping up with the times and the family itself.

Imagine your family getting together for yet another annual gathering in fifty years. What would you like to see the family do? If you have made sure to set the foundation for your legacy family, you will most likely see multiple generations at this annual gathering, no matter where they live. They will know each other, and you will hear conversations on topics related to forwarding the family mission. You will see traditions that welcome new members, and you will see intergenerational mentoring and appreciation. The family branches will know each other because they have a common mission that they continue to strengthen and develop.

Now is the time to define and establish your family's values, purpose, and mission so these will become a practical and philosophical foundation for your legacy family.

7

WHAT IS THE BENEFIT OF HAVING ANNUAL FAMILY MEETINGS?

Profound connections occur when people gather face-to-face. Nothing can replace the energy that builds when people are in one place together, furthering the same cause with trust, support, and a commitment to success. Although this is the preferred environment for conducting annual family meetings, it is not always feasible. Schedules can trump availability, and, with growing families, it can be difficult to plan a meeting without long lead-time.

Families tend to come together when there is a compelling reason, like a wedding, funeral, graduation, or holiday celebration. They are usually centered on a "main event," either one that does not recur, like a wedding, funeral, or graduation, or a tradition, like holiday gatherings. Unless the family has already put in place its purpose and members understand the value of developing it for future members, the family gathering can feel like an obligation instead of like an opportunity to reinforce cohesion.

Therefore, as you create the purpose for your family meeting, consider how you will make attendance enticing for family members who live further away or have schedules that are difficult to coordinate. Sometimes the family matriarch or patriarch will communicate to family members that they have something important to discuss and want everyone present. However, such vague language may cause family members to ask: "What's wrong?" Anxiety may rise. Or, the family matriarch or patriarch might announce that they are reviewing their estate plans and want to include the rest of the family in their planning. Still others might explain that they are looking at ways to keep the family more connected across generations and need to have the family together to initiate steps toward making that happen.

Most family members would not want to miss out on important family discussions, although there will be those who may be prevented from attending by work schedules, medical issues, or other compelling reasons. Perhaps they could "attend" via video-conference. With proper boundaries for expectations on this blend, this type of meeting can be beneficial even if not ideal.

While you must give everyone in your family an opportunity to come to the table and participate, you should also plan to follow up immediately with all attendees to capture feedback. Ask them whether and how they benefited and how they saw the family benefit from the meeting. This is critical for inclusion and for keeping the family bonds tight.

One family I worked with held a family meeting called the "Heads-up Summit." The four children were informed, months earlier, that their parents wanted to formalize the future of the family and discuss what that meant to them. Because two of the adult children were out of the country on business, the first meeting was held with two of the children present at their parents' home and the two others participating through online video conferencing.

This meeting had two major agenda items: 1) a general overview of what the parents wanted to accomplish by having an inclusive in-person meeting, and 2) an exercise to determine their collective family values. Everyone had an opportunity to participate. Because there were rules about how the meeting was to be conducted—no cell phone interruptions, no looking at texts or emails—both the in-person and virtual participation worked well together and the two agenda items were fully addressed. But it was also understood that being together in person would likely have created even greater connection and deeper trust.

A second meeting, about ten months later, was then scheduled at a time and location where all six adult family members could be physically present. The adult children understood how much more meaningful it would be to be present in person to hear their parents' stories about experiencing challenges, setbacks, and successes. They wanted to be together to feel and support each other's contributions as they refined their family's values and collective mission. Although it was difficult for one of the adult children to commit to the date, all attended and were amazed at the difference their presence made. When they could see each other, react to the family dynamics in person, and feel the strong connections they were creating, they could understand on a deeper level the power of the family dynamic. They realized that being in physical proximity clearly made communication easier, with fewer interruptions, distractions, and misunderstandings. They decided to meet annually in person for the next five years.

An in-person meeting should be made a priority. Most importantly, when you decide to convene an in-person family meeting, keep this in mind: you are not imposing on your family. Instead, you are creating a foundation of strong and sustained connection. You are providing your family with the tools to avoid becoming part of the statistic that says that ninety percent of inherited wealth is gone by the end of the third generation. You are creating the cornerstone to a tangible family legacy lasting for, across, and through generations.

You will have created a living inheritance because you hosted that first annual family summit. That will be a huge accomplishment.

8

HOW CAN WE MAKE FAMILY MEETINGS MORE INTERESTING?

There are four elements to a successful, meaningful family meeting:

- A well understood and well communicated purpose for the meeting. This helps foster a level of understanding of what the meeting is for.
- A well thought out and circulated agenda. This provides an opportunity for a feeling of safety. No surprises in the agenda!
- Inclusivity for all attendees. This adds to a feeling of trust that all voices have a place at the meeting, without interruption or derision.
- Dedicated time for both family business and family fun. This allows for relationships to deepen and connections to strengthen.

A meeting framework that incorporates these elements will help frame a meeting in which all know what is to be covered, all are respected for their opinions, and all feel comfortable that there will be time to relax.

Some families compartmentalize their family meetings so that family business, family development activities, and family fun are on separate days. For example, some families carve out a weekend where one day is for business and family development, and the other for family fun.

Some families plan a special celebratory dinner during their weekend retreat, complete with awards, prizes, and other family-developed celebrations. They use these celebrations as opportunities for younger and newer (spouses or significant others) members to learn about the richness of the family, describe a skill or talent they can add to the family skill/talent pool, or pick a family value that means a lot to them and talk about that with the family. A wonderful characteristic of great families is that they find ways to build, develop, and foster their appreciation of each other.

Over time, your meetings may become a little stale. If you find that your typical family meetings have become less attractive and family members are avoiding attending them, you might consider introducing a new meeting paradigm.

For example, you could ask everyone to come prepared to share how a family value has made a difference in their lives, or how they may want to revitalize a family value they see as dormant. You might review the family mission as a group and then have each person talk about how the mission has brought meaning to their lives or how they plan to contribute to its health in the coming year. You might bring in a facilitator to help the family learn about respectful communication, team building, or financial literacy. If your family is involved in philanthropic activities, you might bring in the executive director of an organization that the family supports, or invite the recipient of significant donations the family has made, to discuss how the donation has helped further the vision of that particular organization or recipient. You might form a committee to be responsible for developing imaginative and dynamic topics, activities, and formats for future meetings. These are a few ideas to help stimulate your family meetings.

Get creative, ask for help, try something new, and shake things up! Remember, the heart of your family is its set of shared values. Refer to them every year in ways that matter. Your family's continuing connections will thrive because the why (the values) are the glue to a strong and thriving family.

9

HOW DO WE KEEP OUR NEW FINANCIAL STATUS FROM UNDERMINING FAMILY HARMONY?

Whether you sell a business, sell substantial stock position, win a lottery, sell an idea or patent, or receive an inheritance, it can be tough to deal with new money. Suddenly, you may have more money than many of your friends. Suddenly, you can do things you could not do previously. Suddenly, your world has changed, whether you want it to or not.

Although you may feel the need to act like nothing has changed, everything has indeed changed. Hiding from it or avoiding it is not dealing effectively with it. The question to examine is: How will you maneuver through and manage this sudden change?

Do you tell your friends? Do you tell your relatives? Do you tell your children? If you responded "Yes" to these questions, *what* do you tell them?

When children live in a world that is disconnected from money, they themselves develop a disconnected relationship with money. This is not unusual and is often a result of children modeling what they see and experience in their families. Many children have not been given the proper tools to help them understand the meaning behind the wealth. Instead, they grow up accustomed to the lifestyle wealth is supporting.

Although it may look like it grows on trees, money does not. It can be squandered and spent; it can be saved and invested; or it can be given away or hoarded. Children generally do not understand this. To them, the money is simply … there.

I was introduced to two business partners who had recently sold their company. They each received an initial check for thirty million dollars. One of the men, who I will call "Joe," and his wife, who I will call "Sally," decided that they were going to do the things they had always wanted to do. They bought a penthouse condo downtown. They bought a yacht. They immediately upgraded their cars. Then they started thinking about exclusive vacations they could take, with and without their children. They thought of art and jewelry purchases they could make to add to their new lifestyle. Before their new proceeds were three months old, Joe and Sally had spent eighteen million dollars.

Joe's former partner, who I will call "Mike," was not sure what to do with his new money. His wife—I will call her "Jennifer"—did not want to tell the kids, nor did she want to change their lifestyle… at all. She did not want their friends and neighbors to think differently about them. Mike wanted to buy a new car, as a present to himself, but Jennifer said, "Absolutely not, our cars are fine!" However, she did want to move her elder parents from another state, to be closer by. This would involve purchasing a home for them, but she felt that nobody needed to know who purchased the house. Mike was on board with this idea, but he still wanted his new car. Within a couple of months, financial differences had created new money tensions between Mike and Jennifer. They were at a stalemate regarding the use of their new money. The two offers they made on houses for her parents failed as they fought over the counteroffers. Mike was spending more time away from home, to avoid the financial tension. Their kids felt something was up but spent more time away from home too to avoid getting involved in their parents' issues.

Contrast the stories of Joe and Mike with that of another family I worked with who received a substantial inheritance when a family trust was dissolved.

This third family also felt overwhelmed by the large inheritance they had received. They felt they were over their heads with the prospect of their new fortune and felt some shame about such a lucky break that had come as a result of simply being a beneficiary to a trust. They were referred to me, and their initial conversations were about how to "stay the same when everything had changed due to the vast wealth we've inherited." They lived in a small community in a rural area where money was scarce. They had always felt comfortable in that environment and had avoided money conversations. Money represented different things to each of them and they didn't want to create conflict by talking about their individual views on their money.

Together, they talked about what money meant to their family, what money had been like in their families when they were growing up, what stories they had been told about money, and what they wanted their money to do for them. From there, they felt more capable and eager about determining the purpose of this money for themselves as a family.

They learned how to determine this purpose. This created a framework of distinction between family and personal money. They called the family money the "Gifted Money" and personal money the "Earned Money." This brought a new sense of peace around money, as each bucket and its purpose were defined. As a result of this new understanding, money conversations became easier. Raising topics about money was no longer suspect. Money was merely another important conversation. They had created a clear framework around both buckets, the "Gifted" and the "Earned" money.

This particular family built clear distinctions between the family money and each individual family member's earned money. They agreed on the family money's purpose, which included funding post-graduate degrees, non-accredited courses, down payments for a first home (with limits), costs associated with family meetings, and family philanthropic initiatives. The younger family members knew when and how they could petition for that money.

In another family, education, funding a startup, or advancing a talent were very important. Also, financial support was provided for any family member who wanted to get involved in a meaningful cause. Communally, they formed a philanthropic arm of the family. Doing this impacted the family greatly as they listened to each other's ideas, found common interests, and developed common ground while developing a unified family brand and passion around philanthropy.

There is so much to think about when money becomes a new component in a family. It is important to make new family money part of your family's life, as a respected and supported family system. Otherwise, money may well become the source of division and strife, which will run counter to your intention.

10

HOW CAN WE DEEPEN TRUST WITHIN THE FAMILY?

I once read that trust could be defined in one word: predictability. At first, I accepted that definition. But then, as I looked more closely at trust and my experience with it, I determined that trust involved far more. But what "more" was it? I considered how trust factored in my life and realized that there were additional elements to this powerful word.

Trust is a deeply important component of family harmony and unity. In addition to encompassing predictability, trust also implies confidence in another person. Whether this is due to another person's credibility, sincerity, competence, or manner of relating, confidence in that person is a key aspect of sustained trust.

Another element of trust is motivation. Motivation reveals the intentions, priorities, goals, and needs of an individual. Trust is affected by motivation. If motivation is expressed, suspicions can fade. Conversely, if motivations are hidden or not clearly stated, this can foster mistrust.

A third element is reliability, which is different from predictability. Where predictability infers possibility, reliability is demonstrated by and built upon experience and history. Although trust can be built without this, reliability adds a sense of depth and confidence due to its long-term credibility.

And finally, there is the aspect of authority. When you trust someone you relinquish authority to them. Trust infers bestowing authority as well.

In families who want to pass the baton of leadership and financial stewardship, trust is critical. Often, adult children do not trust their siblings' financial intentions with their parents' money. Adult children may wonder whether another sibling is having side conversations about money with their parents—conversations that may exclude them.

Tensions and anxieties around trust usually remain hidden until something out of the ordinary disturbs the routine of a family. Tension often lies below the surface of routine conversations and interactions.

Let me share a recent incident that illustrates how fragile trust can be in a family.

A Case of Damaged Trust

A gentleman revealed to me that he and his wife had decided to give a substantial cash gift to each of their three adult children. They felt very good about their decision and assumed their adult children would be delighted to receive these unexpected financial gifts. The parents gave each child a check, but before the year had passed, the parents began to question the wisdom of having made these gifts.

Within the first six months, one son came back to his parents and said he and his wife did not want any more financial gifts. His wife, he reported, thought her husband's parents were trying to "buy" their love with the gift. The parents were shocked and the son was embarrassed; but the wife was adamant: no more cash gifts.

The second adult child told her parents that she and her husband had decided they did not want more money until her parents had died. They felt that accepting money would change the relationship with her parents and did not want this to happen. This daughter worried that she and her husband would come to expect more money. She also did not trust her own behavior with money. She had paid off her credit cards and had put some of the parents' gift in savings. But she was already thinking, she said, about what she could buy with it. The gift had inadvertently served to remind her of her own precarious behaviors with money, behaviors she did not always trust.

The third adult child simply never talked about the gift he had received. There was no thank-you and no follow-up. Nothing was ever said about it again.

The painful emotional reaction that the parents had after these responses was not what they had expected at all. As a result of their own reaction, they began to think about what else they might do with their money and where their generosity would be more outwardly appreciated. With deep sadness, the parents now noted that there was a new awkwardness present when they got together with their adult children. The love was there but a level of trust had been severed. The gift of money had created questions about motivation, questions that were never dealt with. The parents wished they could turn back time to before they had made the gifts to their children, back when nothing had been disturbed.

Trust is a key value for families who want to stay unified for now and for future generations. It is supported and nurtured by communication that thrives on understanding, purpose, and empathy. When any of these are interrupted or disturbed, trust weakens.

The Four Keys to Deepening Trust

So, what are the keys to making sure your family does not lose mutual trust when money comes into the picture?

The first key is to have a set of shared family values. These values become the "why" of what you do. In the example above, the value that was important to the parents and the reason they gave sudden big gifts to their children was love—their love for their children. In this case, for them, love meant sharing: The parents felt they wanted to share their money, and the children did not know the "why" behind the gifts, so they, naturally, constructed their own stories about why they were being given sudden gifts of money. Values, when they are revealed, talked about, and outwardly expressed in a family, become a great form of understanding. Values act like a glue keeping the family focused on what is important to them as a cohesive unit. Values become the pillar of trust every family member can lean on, rely on, and utilize to further the family.

One family I worked with felt that merely by *being* a family, they would remain close and connected. I asked the younger adult third-generation members what they thought was the glue that kept them together. They mentioned events like Thanksgiving, holidays, and weddings, in addition to activities like school events, extracurricular games, and special projects. But these could and would be revised as passions and interests changed. Although they felt appreciation for the attention given to them, the younger generation found it increasingly difficult to attend "family events." They were busy with their own lives, their own events. They were concerned that these "family events" would not be enough to keep them together, thriving as an intergenerational community. After experiencing a group exercise that uncovered their common family values, the members felt a deeper sense of belonging, which unified them as a group. This new understanding created a cornerstone of trust built around a shared purpose, well worth developing. Over the years, these shared values became the purpose of their meetings and served as the main ingredient to their deepening trust in their four-generation family.

The second key to trust is having a family mission, a stated, common, communal purpose. When families agree on this communal purpose, they begin to build a strong common foundation. Without an agreed-upon common purpose, competing wants and hidden agendas can emerge. This can lead to weakened trust, as children are not sure where they each stand with their parents, in comparison with their siblings. This can lead to a withdrawing of trust. Trust is weakened when one feels isolated or misunderstood.

Another family I worked with found that their mission statement had grown stale. They brought me in to help revitalize it. Their mission statement was their collective connection, and they were ready to make it more meaningful. They created teams to find ways to make their mission more relevant. When they were done, they added more specificity to what success would look like as they reported on their mission statement at their annual meetings. They added new elements to their mission statement, including the provision of ongoing education to enhance their careers. For one member, this meant developing a family grant to hire a ghost writer to help them complete their award-winning cookbooks. For another family member, it meant providing extra tutoring that would help them feel confident about acing a professional exam the first time they sat for it. And for a third child, it meant being able to give some time and expertise to preparing a startup company for a round of angel investing. There are many ways a family can refresh its purpose.

The third key is the family story. In 2010, Emory University published a study in its online ***Journal of Family Life (March 3, 2010).*** The study was produced by two prominent Emory psychologists, Robyn Fivush and Marshall Duke, and a former graduate student, Jennifer Bohanek. They wanted to understand the impact of family stories on a family's dynamics with their adolescent members.

"Family stories," the researchers wrote, "... help children understand who they are in the world." (read it here: http://shared.web.emory.edu/emory/news/releases/2010/03/children-benefit-if-they-know-about-their-relatives-study-finds.html#.Xpdcu4hKiHs) These unique and important stories help children understand where they come from, in a very different way but akin to the DNA tests available today. Neither of these will tell us who we are going to become, but they do shed light on what brought us here.

The power of these important stories is their experiential transmission of connectivity. Before this study, researchers had an inkling that family stories contributed to a child's well-being and identity but had not measured their ideas. Now there was evidence. The study found that the teenagers in the study expressed "...higher levels of emotional well-being, and also higher levels of identity achievement, even when controlling for general level of family functioning." (read it here: (http://shared.web.emory.edu/emory/news/releases/2010/03/children-benefit-if-they-know-about-their-relatives-study-finds.html#.Xpdcu4hKiHs) People want to feel a connection to where they came from. For a family that wants to stay relevant, significant, and together for generations, a shared history becomes a pillar of common ground, a place where trust resides.

Stories go a long way in building and retaining bonds of trust. They remind families of their commonality and their shared culture. Stories provide the foundation on which trust can be cultivated, evidenced, and developed for generations, toward an understanding of each other. It will be a trust built on experiences understood and shared.

The fourth key is providing dynamic activities that involve members from different generations. A philanthropic initiative is one such activity. A family philanthropic team can research an organization that aligns with the family mission. This team can then provide the family with a report outlining how the family gifts will impact the organization, and what their preferences are for hearing back from the organization. 'Philanthropic initiatives can enhance and promote multigenerational communication, harmony, and trust.

Another possible activity is the building of financial literacy. This can be done in workshop settings, hosted by those who are familiar with money behaviors and their impacts on a life with money. Experiential and exploratory learning work well here. These workshops can be set up using games that provide an avenue to learning. Activities that explore money behaviors can demystify money while teaching children productive money behaviors. These workshops can build valuable communication skills around money. It is important that all members have an opportunity to be heard and to have a voice in these important workshops.

Senior members of a family I worked with were concerned about money habits and behaviors forming in the third and fourth generations. Members of the two younger generations did not fully understand the meaning of the money that the family business was generating. They were using their portions—and requiring more—for their ballooning lifestyles. I was invited to conduct a pair of financial workshops designed to introduce the youngest generation to sound financial behaviors. They learned about money through a game I put together specifically for this family that included consequences, challenges, and rewards resulting from their money choices. It was great fun and they learned much about the impacts of their money choices. When I returned for the second workshop, I introduced them to the 5 S.I.D.E.S. of Money©, a model for **S**aving, **I**nvesting, **D**onating, **E**arning, and **S**pending, through a course meant to establish a foundation of strong financial stewardship. It involves a series of activities that introduced attendees to the various uses of money, the triggers that supported them and the triggers that thwarted them, and ways to master their money behaviors. Each category (Saving, Investing, Donating, Earning, and Spending) was examined and applied to each person's life so they could develop their own models of control over money. The activities were a welcome tool for continued family financial literacy development.

11

WHAT SHOULD WE CONSIDER WHEN HIRING SOMEONE TO GUIDE US IN DEVELOPING OUR FAMILY LEGACY?

It is important that you and your family feel comfortable with the family advisors you bring in. They will be working very closely with you and your family. You will need to trust them, rely on their knowledge, and feel confident that what they say will make a real difference in what you do.

Because they may interact with your attorneys, accountants, financial advisors, and other related professionals, you will want an advisor who can be a liaison between you and the rest of your professional team.

You should look for those who are dedicated to and understand the importance, value, and consequence of what you are looking to achieve. You need to find those who know how to facilitate rather than dictate, and who know how to respect and work with various emotions and dynamics without getting pulled into them. You want someone who can adapt to your unique circumstances, providing you with productive activities. And you want a consultant who can guide and help you build supportive and sustainable family dynamic frameworks.

There are many areas to look at when creating a long-lasting family, unified in its purpose. It requires uncovering your values and developing a purpose and/or mission statement. It means developing a platform of trust, inclusive communication, respect, mentoring, and ongoing family development. It can include building philanthropic initiatives, creating the meaningful family story, and arranging annual family get-togethers that foster unity through diversity. It means navigating through challenging issues with dynamics that encourage involvement rather than division or isolation. Your chosen coach/consultant/facilitator/mediator must be versed in these sensitive areas not only to protect and safeguard your family's love, but also so grow its base and foster its unity.

12

PARTING THOUGHTS

To successfully ensure harmony for generations to come, families need to:

- Understand the purpose of the family as contrasted with the purpose of their individual lives
- Develop a high level of trust among family members through inclusive and effective communication
- Build a foundation that allows the family to come together, unified, in support of its defined mission.

When you put in place the systems, tools, and activities that generate trust and inclusivity—and when you have the framework for an agreed-upon and supported purpose—you and your family will find that you will shift from being a group that thinks about its present to being one that is steeped in its stories of the past, its merits in the present, and its devotion to safeguarding the future of a strong unified family.

Families that have this kind of foundation will find that their successes will be significant gifts to pass from one generation to the next. They will find that instead of being merely consumers of wealth, they will become stewards of it, for generations.

You have a decision to make about what to do as a family.

When you choose to become a legacy family, you are committing to creating, building, and sustaining a significant family community for generations.

When your family purpose and mission, along with deep trust among its members, have been successfully developed, its members can feel confident and proud that the baton of leadership and stewardship will pass successfully from one generation to the next.

You will learn from each other's failures and successes. You will increase the longevity of your family unity, beyond its financial wealth, to encompass purpose, trust, and harmony for generations. This will build a strong family, that, because of the foundation it has built, will have tools to manage the vicissitudes of life, through a common purpose and respectful support of each member.

As you transfer your wisdom with your wealth, may your family strengthen and ensure its longevity.

ABOUT THE AUTHOR

Bhaj Townsend is a leading authority in legacy planning for families. She holds two certificates: as a Fellow of the Heritage Institute, and as a recipient of the Family Heirs Coaching Certificate from The Institute for Preparing Heirs. She is the author of two books, three coaching programs, numerous articles, and many intergenerational projects.

She is the president of the Northwest Family Business Advisors in Seattle, past president of the East King County Estate Planning Council in Seattle, and a recipient of the Who's Who Albert Nelson Marquis Lifetime Achievement Award. She has spoken often (and has been interviewed) on topics pertinent to forming and sustaining legacy families.

Bhaj brings to her work direct experience with the challenges she counsels families about. Her own family experienced the effects of a third-generation breakdown in the family business. The family had built the lifestyle but not the foundation for a successful transfer of the family values and mission to future generations. Because of the tensions and consequences of this circumstance, Bhaj dedicated her professional life to understanding and guiding other families on how to stay connected when money is involved.

In her twenty-year career as a financial planner, Bhaj has had the opportunity to understand that financial stewardship is rare. In the early 1990s she developed her nationally acclaimed Money Focus program to coach people on financial stewardship. Over the years, she saw that money needed to be addressed in the context of family culture just as much as it needed to be addressed with individual people. She, then, incorporated her money-behavior programs into her work with intergenerational family dynamics to deepen their communication about their wealth.

Bhaj is the founder of Focus and Sustain, coaching families since 1997 to strengthen their purpose, relationships, dynamics, and unity over generations. She welcomes your questions.

Made in the USA
Las Vegas, NV
10 January 2021